# THE VERY BEST OF TRADITIONAL
# IRISH COOKING

# THE VERY BEST OF TRADITIONAL
# IRISH COOKING

MORE THAN 60 CLASSIC STEP-BY-STEP DISHES FROM THE EMERALD ISLE,
BEAUTIFULLY ILLUSTRATED WITH OVER 250 PHOTOGRAPHS

BIDDY WHITE LENNON AND
GEORGINA CAMPBELL

southwater

This edition is published by Southwater,
an imprint of Anness Publishing Ltd
Hermes House, 88–89 Blackfriars Road, London SE1 8HA;
tel. 020 7401 2077; fax 020 7633 9499

www.southwaterbooks.com; www.annesspublishing.com

If you like the images in this book and would like to investigate using
them for publishing, promotions or advertising, please visit our
website www.practicalpictures.com for more information.

UK agent: The Manning Partnership Ltd; tel. 01225 478444;
fax 01225 478440; sales@manning-partnership.co.uk

UK distributor: Grantham Book Services Ltd;
tel. 01476 541080; fax 01476 541061; orders@gbs.tbs-ltd.co.uk

North American agent/distributor: National Book Network;
tel. 301 459 3366; fax 301 429 5746; www.nbnbooks.com

Australian agent/distributor: Pan Macmillan Australia;
tel. 1300 135 113; fax 1300 135 103;
customer.service@macmillan.com.au

New Zealand agent/distributor: David Bateman Ltd;
tel. (09) 415 7664; fax (09) 415 8892

ETHICAL TRADING POLICY
Because of our ongoing ecological investment programme, you, as our
customer, can have the pleasure and reassurance of knowing that a
tree is being cultivated on your behalf to naturally replace the materials
used to make the book you are holding. For further information about
this scheme, go to www.annesspublishing.com/trees

Publisher: Joanna Lorenz
Senior Project Editor: Lucy Doncaster
Publishing Assistant: Joel Simons
Photographer: Craig Robertson
Food Stylist: Emma MacIntosh
Prop Stylist: Helen Trent
Designer: Nigel Partridge
Production Controller: Mai Ling Collyer

© Anness Publishing Ltd 2009

Previously published as part of a larger volume,
*The Irish Heritage Cookbook*

PUBLISHER'S NOTE
Although the advice and information in this book are believed to be
accurate and true at the time of going to press, neither the authors nor
the publisher can accept any legal responsibility or liability for any errors or
omissions that may be made nor for any inaccuracies nor for any harm
or injury that comes from following instructions or advice in this book.

NOTES
Bracketed terms are intended for American readers.

For all recipes, quantities are given in metric and imperial measures
and, where appropriate, in standard cups and spoons. Follow one set
of measures, but not a mixture, because they are not interchangeable.

Standard spoon and cup measures are level. 1 tsp = 5ml,
1 tbsp = 15ml, 1 cup = 250ml/8fl oz.

Australian standard tablespoons are 20ml. Australian readers should
use 3 tsp in place of 1 tbsp for measuring small quantities.

American pints are 16fl oz/2 cups. American readers should use
20fl oz/2.5 cups in place of 1 pint when measuring liquids.

Electric oven temperatures in this book are for conventional ovens.
When using a fan oven, the temperature will probably need to be
reduced by about 10–20°C/20–40°F. Since ovens vary, you should
check with your manufacturer's instruction book for guidance.

The nutritional analysis given for each recipe is calculated per portion
(i.e. serving or item), unless otherwise stated. If the recipe gives a
range, such as Serves 4–6, then the nutritional analysis will be for
the smaller portion size, i.e. 6 servings. Measurements for sodium
do not include salt added to taste.

Medium (US large) eggs are used unless otherwise stated.

Front cover shows Dublin Coddle – for recipe, see page 54.

PICTURE CREDITS
All photographs are by Craig Robertson except the following:
Billy Clarke p71. iStock p10b, p11t, p12b, p13t, p14b. Jameson
Irish Whiskey Picture Library p84. Mick Rock p7b. Peter Zoeller p7t.
Seoirse de Luan p77. Stockbyte/Punchstock p24, p30, p32, p40, p48,
p59, p60, p89, p90.

# Contents

# Introduction

From its lush green pastures and rolling arable countryside to its well-stocked waters and centuries-old food industries, Ireland is justly famous for its high-quality produce and rich culinary traditions.

## Geography and climate

Situated on the outermost edge of Europe, the island's western coastline follows the line of Europe's continental shelf, united by the Atlantic Ocean, from Cadiz in the south of Spain to Bergen in Norway. The topography ranges from low central plains to a surrounding ring of mountains, the highest of which is Carrauntoohil, standing at 1041m/3414ft above sea level.

Politically, the country comprises two parts: Northern Ireland, which is a constituent country of the United Kingdom and represents one-sixth of the land; and the Republic of Ireland, which has jurisdiction over the remaining five-sixths of the island.

Blessed with a temperate climate, Ireland is only rarely influenced by the cold of Northern Europe but always, especially along the western seaboard, by the warm, wet westerly winds that blow in over the warm Gulf Stream.

As a result, the climate is extremely varied, especially for a small island, going from sunshine to rain within minutes. Rainfall is high, but variable: 1,400mm/55in in the south and west and less than 700mm/27in in the sunnier south-east. Numerous rainy days and infrequent droughts mean high humidity, which brings cloud cover and so less bright sunshine than in much of Europe.

## A wealth of produce

As a result of its clement climate, Ireland is a fast-growing food-exporting nation, with its tender grass-fed beef and lamb and top-quality dairy produce selling all over the world. You only need to stand in any Irish fishing port to observe how foreign trawlers and fish buyers covet the fresh seafood, caught in clean Atlantic waters.

All over Ireland similar crops are grown and the same foodstuffs produced; however, the best grassland for cattle is in the counties of Kildare, Meath and the Golden Vale, and the best mountain lamb is found in the mountains of Connemara and Wicklow. Wexford and the north of County Dublin on the east coast are famous for producing high-quality soft fruits.

## Ireland's favourite food

The cuisine of Ireland has undergone several changes since the earliest hunter-fisher-gatherers 9000 years ago. Successive waves of farming trends, such as *bánbhianna* (white foods made from milk) and the later introduction of wheat, fruit and vegetable crops by

**Left** There are 32 counties within Ireland and Northern Ireland. Dublin is the capital city of Ireland and other main regional towns include Cork and Galway. Belfast is the capital city of Northern Ireland.

***Left*** *Harvesting cultivated mussels on a fish farm in the clean, clear waters of Killary Harbour, County Galway.*

## Ireland's favourite drink

Prevented by the climate from growing grapes and producing wine, early Irish settlers became expert brewers of distinctive ciders and beers, many of which are famous throughout the world today. In additon to these traditional drinks, the Irish quickly mastered the art of whiskey distillation and today the country produces some of the best whiskeys in the world.

## About this book

This beautiful book provides an inspiring taste of the fabulous dishes that make up the Irish cuisine. From warming soups and delicate appetizers to satisfying main courses, flavoursome side dishes and a range of sweet treats, the traditional recipes reveal the very best that Ireland has to offer in one delightful volume.

Christians, as well as the imports and ideas brought by later settlers, have all made their mark, revealing a willingness by the Irish to take what they like and make it their own.

Despite this, the Irish rarely abandon a favourite food. Still deeply ingrained in Irish society is a love of the native fish, shellfish and the wild plants; the beef and *bánbhianna* of the Celtic period; the grains, fruits and vegetables of the early Christian tradition; and the game birds, animals and fish brought by the Normans. Even the potato, which eventually (when potato blight destroyed the crops) brought the misery of great famines, still has pride of place on every Irish table.

Change is aways welcome, and adaptability is a key feature of the cuisine. A good example of this is the expansion in the number of pork dishes (which were, for many generations, the main fresh source of meat), following the influx of German families around the beginning of the 20th century.

The Irish have always encouraged chefs, home-grown or incomers, and there is a lively restaurant scene. Today, many Irish chefs returning from a stint abroad are inspired to put a new spin on the traditional foods and in doing so offer support to a new wave of speciality food growers and producers.

***Right*** *The pagodas and the warehouse of the Old Bushmills Distillery viewed over the dammed St Columb's Rill, County Antrim, Northern Ireland.*

# Vegetables, herbs and fruits

The Irish have no great tradition of vegetable cookery, but vegetables and potatoes were important in their diet. A limited range of types thrives outdoors: the potato, onion, leek, carrot, parsnip, cabbage, Brussels sprout, cauliflower, swede (rutabaga) – known in Ireland as turnip – and beetroot (beet). Vegetables were usually plain boiled and dressed with butter.

Fresh herbs are widely used in many Irish recipes, imparting their colour and aroma as well their distinctive flavours. Fruits are also popular in a range of sweet and savoury dishes, including pies, tarts, puddings and cold desserts such as mousses.

## Vegetables

In modern Ireland, vegetables are most often served as a mixed side dish. Traditional soups and stews depend upon a high vegetable and herb content but this (and the tradition of one-pot cooking) often led to vegetables being overcooked. Modern transport allows out-of-season vegetables to be imported from many parts of the world, but the Irish still

*Below* Potatoes and carrots are two of the most commonly eaten vegetables.

eagerly await the arrival of home-grown new season's potatoes and field vegetables.

Organic vegetable growing in Ireland is increasing. Growers, countrywide, supply local towns using several ways: wholesale markets, growers' markets, health food stores, farm gate selling and weekly box-delivery systems. Many chefs now source organic vegetables locally.

As well as accompanying main dishes, vegetables are used in soups, in first courses, as garnishes for entrées, as vegetarian dishes, and in many savoury dishes. Carrot, onion,

*Above* Cabbage is the second largest vegetable crop in Ireland.

celery, leek, parsnip, swede, with fresh parsley, thyme, garlic and bay leaf, are known in Ireland as 'pot-herbs' – a basic ingredient in many stews and soups, and as 'the bed' that absorbs juices when roasting red meats.

**Potato** Apart from 'first earlies' such as Homeguard or Ulster Sceptre, the Irish prefer floury potatoes, such as Maris Piper, Golden Wonder and Kerr's Pink. They eat them in huge quantities, boiled or steamed in their skins (removed at table on a side plate) and dressed with butter. Potatoes are also mashed with milk (or cream) and butter, with added herbs or other mashed vegetables. Traditional dishes like boxty, colcannon, poundies, champ, stampy, potato cakes, breads and pastry are popular, and in some restaurants they can contain surprising additions.

**Cabbage** Eaten all year round, cabbage is the largest horticultural crop grown in Ireland after potatoes. Most types are cultivated: white, green and red (when stewed with apple, red cabbage is a favourite accompaniment for goose and venison). The Irish prefer pointed-hearted, fresh, soft green-leafed types. Cabbage can be eaten raw, boiled, steamed and stir-fried.

**Carrot** Irish-grown carrots are available from June until April. Young pencil-thin ones are eaten raw or boiled until just tender, then buttered and sprinkled with fresh parsley.

**Onion, leek and spring onion (scallion)** The Irish adore onions, and they are also an essential cleansing, health-promoting element in their diet. They can be eaten raw in salads, fried in butter, boiled in milk, roasted (often with a cheese topping) or chargrilled.

No Irish person regards beefsteak as correctly presented without a serving of butter-fried onion. Leek is often used with fish in the same way as onion with meat. Spring onions (scallions) are used to flavour traditional potato dishes such as champ or colcannon, and in salads.

**Celery** An essential pot-herb, celery is eaten raw (as crudités), braised (especially the hearts *au gratin*), with cheese or as an ingredient in a soup.

*Below Sun-ripened gooseberries.*

**Parsnip** A sweetener for stews and soups, young parsnips are also eaten blanched or plain roasted. Older ones are boiled, mashed, creamed and often mixed with mashed carrots or turnips. They also make a delicious spiced soup.

**Swede** Known as turnip, the firmer textured, less bitter-tasting swede (rutabaga) is preferred to the white turnip. It is usually served as a mash (with cream and chives) or par-boiled then fried in bacon fat.

**Cauliflower and broccoli** These popular vegetables can be cooked in similar ways. Favourite dishes are the classic *au gratin* and a soup incorporating cheese and cream.

*Below Home-made fruit compote.*

*Left Raspberries – deep red fruits, with a wonderfully intense flavour.*

**Globe artichoke and Jerusalem artichoke** The globe artichoke flourishes in the warmth of the south-west and its hearts are greatly appreciated. Jerusalem artichokes grow easily in Ireland and are used for soup and often added to potato mashes.

## Herbs

Parsley, thyme, chives, basil, sage and mint still remain the most widely used fresh herbs in Irish home cooking, but almost all herbs are commercially grown. Leaves of tansy, a common weed, were once an essential ingredient in black puddings (blood sausage) but are now rarely used in this way.

## Fruits

Raspberries, strawberries, loganberries, blackberries, tayberries, blueberries, fraughans (bilberries), red and blackcurrants, and rhubarb are all commercial crops, which are eaten fresh and now used by artisan producers to make jams, compotes and sauces.

**Apple** This is an important crop for cider-making and eating raw and cooked. The Bramley, fluffy in texture, is generally preferred for cooking.

**Pear** No longer a commercial crop, pears are still available locally.

**Wexford strawberry** Seasonal and luscious, these berries are eaten fresh with cream (sometimes whipped) and a sprinkling of sugar.

**Gooseberry** So named because they 'cut' the fat taste of goose, gooseberries are used to make sauces and chutneys and served with fatty-tasting foods like pork, goose, mackerel and fresh herring.

**Rhubarb** Tart rhubarb is used in the same way as gooseberries as well as in a range of tarts, crumbles and pies.

# Fish and shellfish

The seas around Ireland are rich and heavily fished by fleets from many other countries. Not all the fish caught are landed in Ireland but many are eagerly bought for immediate export to the capitals of Europe. In the better Irish restaurants, some specializing in fish, there is usually a fish 'special of the day' – outside Dublin this usually means that it has been caught locally and landed in the last 24 hours.

Non-migratory freshwater fish, such as pike, perch, carp and bream, are not native to Ireland and were, in the main, introduced by the Normans. Known as 'coarse' fish, they are not really rated by the Irish and nowadays are rarely eaten.

Migratory fish, such as salmon, white (sea) trout and eels, are highly prized. When an Irishman asks an angler if he has caught 'a fish' he does not mean any fish, he means a salmon – a usage found in written sources as far back as early in the 10th century.

On the whole, Irish people prefer their fish simply cooked, sometimes served with classic (mainly French) sauces. In restaurants, however, fish and shellfish, such as crab, lobster, crayfish and Dublin Bay prawns (jumbo shrimp), are usually treated with greater imagination by

**Below** *Fly-fishing is a popular hobby in all parts of Ireland.*

many chefs. Fishcakes, fish pâtés, terrines and galantines feature widely on menus and will often be served with spicy international-style jams and salsas.

There is no great tradition of fish soups, but one, universally known as seafood chowder, is widely available and much enjoyed in pubs at lunchtime. There is no standard recipe, but a good one can be truly sublime and may contain anything from white fish and salmon to shellfish, prawns (shrimp), crab claw, mussels, clams, scallops or scallop corals, and sometimes even tiny rings of baby squid and matchsticks of crisp bacon.

## Freshwater fish

**Salmon (*bradán*)** Fresh salmon appears on the menu of almost every Irish wedding, restaurant and party. It is usually poached whole with butter, white wine or cider and herbs, such as dill or fennel leaves. If served cold, the skin is often replaced by overlapping, paper-thin slices of cucumber. Whole, cooked farmed salmon is available in supermarkets. Most restaurants will serve salmon steaks (*darns*), sometimes briefly marinated, then pan-seared. Buttered baby new potatoes with watercress or wilted baby spinach leaves with a wine and cream-based sauce are a classic accompaniment.

**Sea (white) trout (*breac geal*)** Because of its increasing scarcity, this migratory trout is currently even more highly prized than the salmon. It is always lightly poached with dill.

**Brown (river) trout (*breac*)** There is no better breakfast or supper than one of these freshly caught fish. They are simply gutted, dusted in seasoned flour and pan-fried whole in butter for a quick meal.

**Above** *Atlantic salmon has fatty, deep pink flesh with a superb, rich flavour.*

## Sea fish

Turbot (turband) and black sole (*sól*) are the Irish favourites; but brill (*broit*), megrim (*scoilteán*), white sole (*leathóg bhán*), lemon sole (*leathóg mhín*) and plaice or flounder (*leathóg ballach*) are all popular; the last two are frequently offered for breakfast. They are usually cooked in butter, and offered whole on the bone or filleted, and served with a herb or lemon-based sauce.

**Mackerel (*ronnach*)** An Irish favourite whole or filleted, mackerel are usually pan-fried fresh and served with a gooseberry sauce. Fillets are now regularly hot-smoked by artisan producers.

**Herring (*scadán*)** The Irish do everything to the herring that their northern European neighbours do. Traditionally, fresh fillets are coated in crushed oatmeal and pan-fried in butter. Many are kippered (cured and smoked).

**Tuna (*tuinnín*)** Albacore and bluefin tuna are often cut into thick 'steaks', pan-seared and served with a sauce.

**Ray (*roc*)** Ray wings are a great Irish favourite (even in takeaway meals); they are most often simply seasoned, floured, pan-fried and served with a nutty black butter or caper sauce.

**Monkfish (*láimhineach*)** Popular and widely available, meaty monkfish tail fillets are simply cooked and served with a sauce.

**Hake (*colmóir*)** A great favourite with Irish chefs, hake is expensive because most of the catch is exported to the rest of Europe.

## Shellfish

The Irish eat any shellfish that comes their way with great relish, including clams, winkles, whelks, cockles, limpets, sea urchins, crabs, mussels, oysters, squid, Dublin Bay prawns (jumbo shrimp), crayfish, lobsters and scallops. Many of these are exported in very large quantities to the capitals of Europe, with the result that most of them are now expensive luxury foods in Ireland.

**Lobster** Among the many shellfish dishes there is a classic lobster meal called The Dublin Lawyer, and the joke is that 'you'd need to be a lawyer to afford lobster'! This traditional Irish dish involves serving hot lobster in a cream sauce flavoured with flamed whiskey

**Dublin Bay prawn** Despite its name, the Dublin Bay prawn (jumbo shrimp) is not unique to Dublin Bay at all. It is usually fished in the Irish Sea and is actually a widely distributed species (*Nephrops norvegicus*) known as the Norway lobster, or langoustine. Most restaurants serve them as a first course, cooked in the shell (or removed from the shell and coated in breadcrumbs) with a tasty chilli jam or other fusion-style accompaniments.

**Molluscs** Even though they are exported in vast quantities, mussels and oysters are probably the most enjoyed and plentiful shellfish in Ireland today, as they were in the past.

*Below* Dublin Bay prawns and scallops are very popular in Ireland.

*Above* Many fishing villages, such as this one in County Kerry, still thrive.

Mussels and the non-native Pacific oyster are now extensively cultivated and are enjoyed everywhere, usually cooked in the shell in an unthickened white wine, cream and garlic 'broth', sprinkled with parsley and eaten with wholemeal (whole-wheat) brown soda bread and butter.

Oysters are mostly eaten raw, usually from the shell, with just a squeeze of lemon, or maybe a splash of Tabasco sauce, and traditionally accompanied by a pint of stout. The opening of the native oyster season (September to April) is celebrated annually in Galway. Thousands of oysters are consumed, and countless pints downed during one riotous week. The farmed Pacific oyster is available almost all year round.

Scallops are a great favourite and appear on many menus. The corals, once removed, are now prized, and this delicately flavoured muscle is usually just flash-fried or briefly poached and served with a wide variety of sauces.

## Smoked salmon

Smoked wild Atlantic salmon is a premium product. The cure is mild (about 3 per cent salt) and the fish is cold-smoked. Wild salmon is almost always sold as a whole side fillet, vacuum-packed rather than pre-sliced. To be sure of getting the genuine product and value for money (because it is more costly than farmed salmon) look for the words 'Wild Irish' on the label.

'Irish Smoked Salmon' usually denotes farmed salmon, which is cheaper and often sold pre-sliced. Farmed salmon can, however, be of very high quality, especially if it is certified as organic and farmed in cages far out in the ocean where they develop a firm texture from swimming against the current.

Smoked salmon is commonly served simply with sliced lemon, ground black pepper and wholemeal (whole-wheat) bread and butter, as a light meal or appetizer, but it is also used as an ingredient in many dishes. Salmon is also sometimes cured as gravadlax, or hot-smoked and called 'barbecued salmon'.

# Meat and poultry

Ireland's meat and poultry produce is renowned for its variety and traditions; whether a hearty home-made oxtail stew or a tasty beef fillet from the local sire, a traditional Irish feast from one Irish kitchen is rarely the same as the next. From the countless Kerry cattle dotted along the fields around Killarny, to the lean Connemara mountain lamb of the west coast, local chefs are seldom short of choice cuts.

## Beef

The dairy industry in Ireland has meant that the main source of calves for beef production is from the national cow herd. Two broad types of beef cattle have emerged: lean, late-maturing beef bred from Continental sires (Charolais, Simmental, Limousin, Blonde d'Aquitaine); and early-maturing beef, well-marbled with fat and much tastier, bred from Hereford, Angus and shorthorn sires. The Irish, disliking the lean, dry meat of Continental breeds, particularly appreciate the red, marbled beef of the Hereford and Angus sires.

For the Irish dining out, a thick, juicy steak is the heart of a good dinner and no restaurant, however creative its chef, would dare omit a simply cooked beefsteak (fillet, T-bone, or sirloin) from its menu. The Irish attitude to beef is very sensible: if the beef is good enough it needs no embellishment.

In the home, the Irish eat beef (and other meats) two ways: quickly dry-cooked or slowly wet-cooked. Dishes that are dry-cooked include rib and sirloin roasts, which are often served with a sauce of horseradish, slaked with cream to temper its fiery flavour. Steaks and home-made beefburgers are accompanied by pan-fried mushrooms and onions.

Slow-cooked wet dishes include winter warmers, such as a stew of shin (shank) of beef with stout and root vegetables. Oxtail stew and soup, steak and kidney puddings, and steak and oyster pie are also popular. Ox tongue is delicious lightly brined, slow-cooked with pot-herbs, then skinned, rolled, pressed and eaten cold. New additions to the wet-cooked repertoire include slow-cooked minced (ground) meat sauces to eat with pasta, and lean strips of beef stir-fried Asian-style.

*Left* A pair of Angus fillet steaks.

## Goat and sheep

The sheep kept by early settlers in Ireland are thought to have been dark-fleeced antecedents of the Soay breed, which provided wool by moulting. In addition to sheep, it is likely that goats rather than cows were the primary grazing animal of early farmers, and wild goats still roam the Burren in County Clare.

Curiously, goat kid (young male goat) meat, which was traditionally the meat used to make the famous Irish stew, fell from favour many years ago, although there are some quite large herds kept and bred for milk and farmhouse cheesemaking. However, there has been a quite recent development: the organic feeding of young male goats for supply to specialist restaurants.

Mint, thyme and marjoram are the common herbs used to add flavour to Irish lamb dishes, including stews, chops, steaks, lamb-burgers and speciality sausages. Irish lamb is becoming ever more highly regarded among those who place a high value on naturally reared meat that has a fine flavour because the animal has grazed on hill pastures. In restaurants, menus usually name the hills on which the lamb to be served has been reared.

Preparation still remains simple. The most frequently featured dishes are slow-cooked lamb shanks or rump of lamb, and fast-cooked rack of lamb, often with a herb crust, served with intense sauces flavoured with red wine or port and redcurrants or other berries.

*Left* Ancient breeds of upland sheep in Ireland provide wonderful meat.

***Above*** *Free-range and organic chickens have the best flavour.*

## Pork

Traditionally, every family that could afford it would keep their own pig. Now the production and rearing are done by large-scale manufacturers, artisan producers and specialist butchers specializing in pork.

Fresh and cured, pork could be eaten at every meal of the day. Breakfast, known as 'the full Irish' in southern Ireland, and 'an Ulster fry' in Northern Ireland, consists of bacon, sausages, black pudding (blood sausage) and/or white pudding, served with tomatoes, mushrooms, potato cakes and wholemeal (whole-wheat) soda bread. Ham, salamis, brawn and haslet feature in lunchtime sandwiches.

At dinner, pâtés, terrines and black pudding are served as first courses. Main dishes include chops, roasted loin leg and belly, boiled (and then baked) ham and bacon. Ham and bacon are also used as ingredients to flavour salads, stuffings, mashed potato dishes and even bread.

## Game

Native Irish people have rarely hunted animals for sport; most today are reluctant to kill any creature (except for food) that does not pose a threat to crops or livestock.

Game originally included river fish, shellfish, birds, deer, boar, wild cattle, sheep and goats, as well as wolves, badgers, foxes, wild cats, martens, otters, hares, rabbits and squirrels. The tradition of seasonal 'huntin', shootin' and fishin' for game' within great estates became part of mainly upper-class Irish life during the 18th and 19th centuries.

Today, farmed venison is available all year round in Irish supermarkets and butchers, as steaks, chopped for stewing or in speciality sausages both fresh and smoked.

## Poultry

**Chicken** The Irish were once relatively conservative when using chicken, content with a Sunday roast of stuffed chicken accompanied by boiled bacon and served with a bread sauce. Older hens, with their laying days behind them, used to be stewed with root vegetables or made into pies, but that was in the days when chickens ranged freely about the farmyard, fed on a variety of foods, grew slowly and developed a complex flavour.

Today, intensively reared, industrially produced chicken dominates the market and has become a cheap, weekday, fast-food (usually pre-prepared) option. Organic, free-range farm chickens are available from good supermarkets, craft butchers and farmers' markets but are now an expensive treat. Smoked chicken, a fairly recent innovation, is used as a tasty appetizer.

**Duck** Traditionally, a duck was cooked with turnips, parsley and juniper berries, and apples were often made into a sauce to accompany it. A real farmyard duck is relatively rare now, although excellent ducks are sold by medium and small producers. Smoked duck has become a popular restaurant first course. Fresh duck, cooked so that the skin is crisp and served with a variety of fruity sauces, remains popular in the home. In restaurants the leg is often served as a slow-cooked confit; the breast usually gets brief but high-heat cooking so that it remains rare and juicy.

**Turkey** The turkey was known in Ireland as early as the 17th century. Only in the 20th century, however, did it become the bird of choice for the Christmas dinner and oust the goose as the farmyard bird most likely to generate a good income. This is curious because turkeys are difficult to rear and more prone to disease than geese. Farmhouse, free-range turkeys are highly prized at Christmas, but intensive (industrial) production means that turkey remains a plentiful, cheap and popular white meat.

**Goose** In medieval times goose was stuffed with herbs and fruit, boiled with dumplings and served with apple or garlic sauce. In later times it was roasted, stuffed with onions, bacon and potatoes. There is no great industrial production of geese today, but artisan produced geese are making a come-back as the bird for a special festive occasion.

***Below*** *Goose is an Irish mainstay for festive occasions.*

# Dairy

As one of Ireland's major industries, dairy farming shapes the countryside, permanently covering much of the land in lush green pasture. Despite its small size, the island has diverse microclimates. The south and west are warmed by the Gulf Stream and have quite distinct plants from those in the sunny south-east, and they are different again from the rich 'golden vale' of the southern midlands or of the Drumlin country, the northerly midlands.

It is the country's abundance of grass that gives such consistent high quality to milk and butter, and the variation in herbage which enables so many varieties of cheese, each with a distinctive flavour, to be produced.

## Milk and buttermilk

Full-fat (whole) milk is an essential ingredient in Irish cooking. It is produced by dairy farmers and collected daily by large co-operative creameries for pasteurization and distribution to retailers. Irish milk is not usually subjected to ultra-heat treatment so it retains its fresh flavour and is widely enjoyed as a drink.

Originally, buttermilk was the liquid squeezed out of cream churned for butter. It has a slightly sour flavour as a result of the ripening of the cream.

Natural buttermilk, once a popular drink, is now mainly used for making products such as soft cheese. Cultured buttermilk is fermented with the same organisms used to 'ripen' cream for butter. It is heat-treated to kill bacteria and stop fermentation, which means it doesn't taste so good to drink.

Although buttermilk is no longer drunk as a thirst-quencher or used as a traditional dressing for potatoes, Ireland has a high consumption of buttermilk because it remains an essential ingredient in cooking. It is used by bakers for Irish soda breads and scones, and for the home-baking of bread.

## Butter

Always found on an Irish table, butter is lavishly used on bread, vegetables and cakes. Produced predominantly in large-scale creameries across the country, Irish butter has an excellent flavour and colour. For centuries brand names such as Kerrygold have been exported in vast quantities across Europe.

Available salted or unsalted, creamery butter is regularly sold alongside country (or farm) butter, a variation flavoured by local grasses and given a longer ripening period.

## Cream and yogurt

Two types of cream are available: fresh and soured. Fresh cream – double (heavy) and single (light) – is by far the most popular, and large quantities are

*Left Cows feed on the lush pastures of Ireland, producing high-quality milk.*

*Left Gubbeen is a washed-rind cheese with a scented mushroom flavour and a firm, smooth texture.*

consumed on porridge, in coffee and poured over fruit tarts and desserts. Sour cream is used less, but is occasionally mixed with herbs to dress baked potatoes. Crème fraîche is catching on and is much in evidence in leading restaurants.

As yogurt is not a traditional Irish food, its production is a fairly recent development. However, it is a product in tune with the Irish penchant for fermented and sour-milk products and it is very popular.

## Cheese

Much appreciated as a gourmet ready-to-eat food, farmhouse cheeses such as Ardrahan, Gubbeen or Abbey Blue are frequently eaten as a snack or lunch, or used to add flavour and texture to traditional and contemporary dishes. A good plate of locally selected cheese takes pride of place as a final dinner course eaten with bread, crackers or crisp oatcakes and accompanied by celery, pears, apples, grapes or chutney.

Each cheese is unique to the individual cheesemaker, and several Irish farmhouse cheeses have won awards at international food competitions. This exposure has extended their market to many countries of the world, where they are available in gourmet food outlets and from specialist cheesemongers.

There are a number of established artisan cheesemakers. Some make a single farmhouse cheese, others several varieties. All use the milk from their own herd of cows, sheep or goats, or milk from neighbouring farms.

# Baking

Home-baking has always been popular, and many people still enjoy making a range of breads, cakes and bakes, including barm brack (with fruits and spices), griddle breads, potato cakes, crumpets, muffins and fruit tarts, as well as traditional sweet cakes, such as porter cake, carrot cake and gingerbread (which is a cake, despite its name).

Traditional recipes have been handed down from generation to generation, kept alive in part by baking competitions at local agricultural shows and the work of the Irish Country Women's Association, whose members pass on traditional recipes and baking skills.

### Leavening

Most Irish bread was leavened either with barm (a by-product of brewing), sowans (fermented from oat husks), potato barm sourdough or yeast. Towards the end of the 18th century, however, bicarbonate of soda (baking soda) arrived. Used with buttermilk or soured milk, the action of one enhances the other; bicarbonate of soda interacts with the lactic acid of buttermilk to release carbon dioxide into the dough, making it rise.

Visitors love the taste and texture of Irish bread, and to this day wholemeal (whole-wheat) soda bread remains the bread of the nation. In many parts of Ireland a loaf of this bread is called a 'cake', going back to the old Viking word for a flattish round of bread, *kake* or *kaak*.

*Above* A selection of Irish soda breads and scones.

Although wholemeal soda bread (also called brown bread) is the most popular, the same leavening combination is used for white soda breads, white and brown scones, and sweet teabreads.

### Other ingredients

Dairy foods, the *bánbhianna* of ancient times, are essential in baking. Butter is still traditional, and only for economic reasons will any other fat be substituted. It is used in almost everything, and some cooks even add a small amount to soda bread. Butter is always served with bread, barm brack, scones, teabreads and even porter cake. Hard cheeses are added to bread and scones, and soft fresh cheese is used in baked curd- and cheesecakes. Cream is served with tarts and puddings.

A wide variety of flavouring liquids are used. Buttermilk is used for breads, scones and some cakes; fresh (sweet) milk for cakes, pancakes and puddings. Porter cake, a robust fruitcake, is named after the liquid used: a dark brown, hopped and malty alcoholic drink. Cider (hard) is used in some sponge cakes and puddings. Whiskey is an essential ingredient in the rich, double-iced fruitcakes made for christenings and weddings and in Christmas cake and Christmas pudding (the latter usually contains stout as well).

Crystallized fruits are widely used, mainly lemon, orange, cherry and angelica stems. Dried fruits such as currants, raisins, sultanas (golden raisins), apricots, figs and prunes are also popular.

Fresh fruits used in tarts and cakes include cooking and eating apples, rhubarb, pears, blackberries, strawberries, raspberries and *fraughans* (bilberries or wild blueberries), cranberries, lemons and oranges. Nuts, particularly almonds, hazelnuts and walnuts, are used in everything from bread to cakes and meringues.

As for spices, the most common are cloves, nutmeg, cinnamon, ginger, vanilla and caraway. Most sugar is made from sugar beet, but dark cane sugar, treacle (molasses) and honey are also used.

*Left* Barm brack is one of Ireland's most delicious teabreads.

# Breakfasts, appetizers and light meals

A traditional Irish breakfast ranges from warming porridge and freshly-baked potato cakes to more substantial meals that may include bacon, eggs, sausages, pancakes, fish or kidneys. Lunch or a light supper often comprises a hearty soup, a 'meal in a bowl' that may contain meat or fish, or a tasty snack, which can also be served as an appetizer for a more formal meal.

# Porridge

One of Ireland's oldest foods, porridge remains a favourite way to start the day, especially during winter. Brown sugar or honey, cream and a tot of whiskey are treats added for weekend breakfasts and to spoil guests in some of the best guesthouses and hotels.

**Serves 4**

1 litre/1¾ pints/4 cups water

115g/4oz/1 cup pinhead oatmeal

good pinch of salt

**Variation** Modern rolled oats can be used, in the proportion of 115g/4oz/ 1 cup rolled oats to 750ml/1¼ pints/ 3 cups water, plus a sprinkling of salt. This cooks more quickly than pinhead oatmeal. Simmer, stirring to prevent sticking, for about 5 minutes. Either type of oatmeal can be left to cook overnight in the slow oven of a range.

**1** Put the water, pinhead oatmeal and salt into a heavy pan and bring to the boil over a medium heat, stirring with a wooden spatula. When the porridge is smooth and beginning to thicken, reduce the heat to a simmer.

**2** Cook gently for about 25 minutes, stirring occasionally, until the oatmeal is cooked and the consistency smooth.

**3** Serve hot with cold milk and extra salt, if required.

**Per portion** Energy 115kcal/488kJ; Protein 3.6g; Carbohydrate 20.9g, of which sugars 0g; Fat 2.5g, of which saturates 0g; Cholesterol 0mg; Calcium 16mg; Fibre 2g; Sodium 304mg

# Potato cakes

This is the traditional method of making potato cakes on a griddle or heavy frying pan. Commercial versions are available as thin, pre-cooked cakes, which are fried for breakfast or high tea. Griddle-cooked potato cakes were traditionally buttered and eaten hot with sugar.

**Makes about 12**

675g/1½lb floury potatoes, peeled

salt

25g/1oz/2 tbsp unsalted butter

about 175g/6oz/1½ cups plain (all-purpose) flour

**1** Boil the potatoes in a large pan until tender, then drain well and mash. Salt well, then mix in the butter and allow to cool a little.

**2** Turn out on to a floured work surface and knead in about one-third of its volume in flour, or as much as is needed to make a pliable dough. It will become easier to handle as the flour is incorporated, but avoid overworking it.

**3** Roll out the dough to a thickness of about 1cm/½in and cut into triangles of about equal size.

**4** Heat a dry griddle or heavy frying pan over a low heat and cook the potato cakes on it for about 3 minutes on each side until browned. Serve hot with butter, or sugar, if you prefer.

*Right* From top to bottom, Avalanche, a white-skinned early maincrop potato from Northern Ireland; Avondale, a beige-skinned maincrop from Ireland; and Barna, a red-skinned late maincrop from Ireland.

Per cake Energy 106kcal/449kJ; Protein 2.5g; Carbohydrate 20.8g, of which sugars 0.6g; Fat 2.0g, of which saturates 1.1g; Cholesterol 4.4mg; Calcium 23.5mg; Fibre 1.2g; Sodium 16.9mg

# Oatmeal pancakes with bacon

These oaty pancakes have a special affinity with good bacon, making an interesting base for an alternative to the big traditional fry-up. Serve with traditional or home-made sausages, fried or poached eggs and cooked tomatoes.

**Makes 8 pancakes**

115g/4oz/1 cup fine wholemeal (whole-wheat) flour

25g/1oz/¼ cup fine pinhead oatmeal

pinch of salt

2 eggs

about 300ml/½ pint/1¼ cups buttermilk

butter or oil, for greasing

8 bacon rashers (strips)

**Cook's tip** When whole oats are chopped into pieces they are called pinhead or coarse oatmeal. They take longer to cook than rolled oats and have a chewier texture.

**1** Mix the flour, oatmeal and salt in a large bowl or food processor, beat in the eggs and gradually pour in just enough of the buttermilk to make a thick, creamy batter.

**2** Thoroughly heat a griddle or cast-iron frying pan over a medium-hot heat. When very hot, grease lightly with butter or oil.

**3** Pour in the batter, about a ladleful at a time. Tilt the pan around to spread evenly and cook for about 2 minutes on the first side, or until set and the underside is browned. Turn over and cook for 1 minute until browned.

**4** Keep the pancakes warm while you cook the others. Fry the bacon. Roll the pancakes with a cooked rasher to serve.

**Per pancake** Energy 202kcal/845kJ; Protein 11.9g; Carbohydrate 13.1g, of which sugars 2g; Fat 11.8g, of which saturates 4.8g; Cholesterol 87mg; Calcium 59mg; Fibre 1.5g; Sodium 654mg

# Buttermilk pancakes

These little pancakes are made with buttermilk, which is widely available in Ireland, and they are quite similar to the dropped scones that are so familiar across the water in Scotland. They are delicious served warm from the pan, with honey.

**Makes about 12**

225g/8oz/2 cups plain (all-purpose) flour

7.5ml/1½ tsp bicarbonate of soda (baking soda)

25–50g/1–2oz/2–4 tbsp sugar

1 egg

about 300ml/½ pint/1¼ cups buttermilk

butter and oil, mixed, or white vegetable fat (shortening), for frying

honey, to serve

**1** In a food processor or a large mixing bowl, mix together the plain flour, the bicarbonate of soda and enough sugar to taste. Add the egg, mixing together, and gradually pour in just enough of the buttermilk to make a thick, smooth batter.

**2** Heat a heavy pan and add the butter and oil, or white fat. Place spoonfuls of the batter on to the hot pan and cook for 2–3 minutes until bubbles rise to the surface. Flip the pancakes over and cook for a further 2–3 minutes. Remove from the pan and serve warm with honey.

**Per pancake** Energy 121kcal/508kJ; Protein 3.2g; Carbohydrate 17.9g, of which sugars 3.6g; Fat 4.6g, of which saturates 1.6g; Cholesterol 25mg; Calcium 57.9mg; Fibre 0.6g; Sodium 18.3mg

# Jugged kippers

The demand for naturally smoked kippers is ever increasing. They are most popular for breakfast, served with scrambled eggs, but they're also good at an old-fashioned high tea. Jugging is the same as poaching, except that the only equipment needed is a jug and kettle. Serve with freshly made soda bread or toast and a wedge of lemon, if you like.

**Serves 4**

4 kippers (smoked herrings), preferably naturally smoked, whole or filleted

25g/1oz/2 tbsp butter

ground black pepper

**1** Select a jug (pitcher) tall enough for the kippers to be immersed when the water is added. If the heads are still on, remove them.

**2** Put the fish into the jug, tails up, and then cover them with boiling water. Leave for about 5 minutes, until tender.

**3** Drain well and serve on warmed plates with a knob (pat) of butter and a little black pepper on each kipper.

**Per portion** Energy 449kcal/1859kJ; Protein 31.8g; Carbohydrate 0g, of which sugars 0g; Fat 35.7g, of which saturates 8.3g; Cholesterol 123mg; Calcium 96mg; Fibre 0g; Sodium 1.5g

# Kidney and mushroom toasts

The traditional Irish breakfast treat of lamb's kidneys is most often encountered in the country or regional towns. This little dish makes an excellent alternative to the big 'breakfast plate', or could be a light, tasty supper. Serve with tomato slices or wedges and parsley on hot herby-buttered toast or scones.

**Serves 2–4**

4 large, flat field (portabello) mushrooms, stalks trimmed

75g/3oz/6 tbsp butter

10ml/2 tsp Irish wholegrain mustard

15ml/1 tbsp chopped fresh flat leaf parsley

4 lamb's kidneys, skinned, halved and cored

4 thick slices of brown bread, cut into rounds and toasted, or halved, warm scones

tomato wedges, to serve

sprig of parsley, to garnish

**1** Wash the mushrooms thoroughly and gently remove the stalks.

**2** Blend the butter, wholegrain mustard and fresh parsley together.

**3** Rinse the prepared lamb's kidneys well under cold running water, and pat dry with kitchen paper.

**4** Melt about two-thirds of the butter mixture in a large frying pan and fry the mushrooms and kidneys for about 3 minutes on each side. When the kidneys are cooked to your liking, spread with the remaining herb butter.

**5** Serve with the tomato, garnished with parsley, on the hot toast or scones.

**Per portion** Energy 593kcal/2480kJ; Protein 39.2g; Carbohydrate 26.3g, of which sugars 2.7g; Fat 37.7g, of which saturates 21.6g; Cholesterol 647mg; Calcium 145mg; Fibre 4.3g; Sodium 773mg

# Potato soup

This most Irish of all soups is not only excellent as it is, but versatile too, as it can be used as a base for numerous other soups. Use a floury potato, such as Golden Wonder, and try adding cabbage, leeks or pieces of crispy bacon for a variation.

**2** Add the potatoes to the pan, and mix well with the butter and onions. Season with salt and pepper, cover and cook without colouring over a gentle heat for about 10 minutes. Add the stock, bring to the boil and simmer for 20–30 minutes, until the vegetables are tender.

**3** Remove from the heat and allow to cool slightly. Purée in batches in a blender or food processor. Reheat over a low heat and adjust the seasoning. If the soup seems too thick, add a little extra stock or milk. Serve very hot, sprinkled with chopped chives.

**Below** *Verdant Irish landscape, with fields of lush, agricultural land seen in the view across the gap on Mamore, on the Inishowen peninsula.*

**Serves 6–8**

50g/2oz/¼ cup butter

2 large onions, finely chopped

675g/1½lb potatoes, diced

sea salt and ground black pepper

about 1.75 litres/3 pints/7½ cups hot chicken stock

a little milk, if necessary

chopped fresh chives, to garnish

**1** Melt the butter in a large heavy pan and add the onions, turning them in the butter until well coated. Cover and leave to sweat over a very low heat.

**Per portion** Energy 178kcal/746kJ; Protein 3.5g; Carbohydrate 26.1g, of which sugars 5.4g; Fat 7.4g, of which saturates 4.3g; Cholesterol 18mg; Calcium 29mg; Fibre 2.6g; Sodium 328mg

# Brotchán foltchep

This traditional leek and oatmeal soup is also known as *brotchán roy* and combines leeks, oatmeal and milk – three ingredients that have been staple foods in Ireland for centuries. Serve with freshly baked bread and Irish butter.

**Serves 4–6**

about 1.2 litres/2 pints/5 cups chicken stock and milk, mixed

30ml/2 tbsp medium pinhead oatmeal

6 large leeks, sliced into 2cm/¾in pieces

25g/1oz/2 tbsp butter

sea salt and ground black pepper

pinch of ground mace

30ml/2 tbsp chopped fresh parsley

single (light) cream and chopped fresh parsley leaves or chives, to garnish

**4** Season with salt, pepper and mace, stir in the parsley and serve in warmed bowls.

**5** Add a swirl of cream to the soup and garnish with some chopped fresh parsley leaves or chives, if you like. Serve immediately.

**Variation** You can make nettle soup using this recipe. Pick them in the spring, when the nettle tops are young and tender. Wearing gloves, strip about 10oz/275g nettle tops from the stems, chop them and add to the leeks. Continue as above.

**1** Bring the stock and milk mixture to the boil over medium heat and sprinkle in the oatmeal. Stir well to prevent lumps forming, and then simmer gently.

**2** Wash the leeks in a bowl. Melt the butter in a separate pan and cook the leeks over a gentle heat until they have softened slightly, then add them to the stock mixture.

**3** Simmer for a further 15–20 minutes, or until the oatmeal is cooked. Extra stock or milk can be added if the soup is too thick.

**Per portion** Energy 199kcal/834kJ; Protein 10g; Carbohydrate 19.5g, of which sugars 12.4g; Fat 9.6g, of which saturates 5.1g; Cholesterol 22mg; Calcium 243mg; Fibre 5.8g; Sodium 219mg

# Three-fish terrine

This attractive striped terrine uses haddock, salmon and turbot – all native fish to Irish seas and rivers. Serve with a small salad, freshly made brown bread or Melba toast and butter.

**Serves 8–10**

450g/1lb spinach

350–450g/12oz–1lb haddock, cod or other white fish, skinned and chopped

3 eggs

115g/4oz/2 cups fresh breadcrumbs

300ml/½ pint/1¼ cups fromage blanc

salt and ground black pepper

a little freshly grated nutmeg

350–450g/12oz–1lb fresh salmon fillet

350–450g/12oz–1lb fresh turbot fillet, or other flat fish

oil, for greasing

lemon wedges and sprigs of fresh dill or fennel, to garnish

**1** Preheat the oven to 160°C/325°F/ Gas 3. Remove the stalks from the spinach and cook the leaves briskly in a pan without any added water, shaking the pan occasionally, until the spinach is just tender. Drain and squeeze out the excess water.

**2** Put the spinach into a food processor or blender with the haddock or other white fish, eggs, breadcrumbs, fromage blanc, salt, pepper and nutmeg to taste. Process until smooth.

**3** Skin and bone the salmon fillet and cut it into long thin strips. Repeat with the turbot.

**4** Oil a 900g/2lb loaf tin (pan) or terrine and line the base with a piece of oiled baking parchment or foil, cut to fit. Make layers from the spinach mixture and the strips of salmon and turbot, starting and finishing with the spinach.

**5** Press down carefully and cover with lightly oiled baking parchment. Prick a few holes in it, then put the terrine into a roasting pan and pour enough boiling water around it to come two-thirds of the way up the sides.

**6** Bake in the preheated oven for 1–1½ hours, or until risen, firm and set. Leave to cool, then chill well before serving.

**7** To serve, ease a sharp knife down the sides to loosen the terrine and turn the terrine on to a flat serving dish. Using a sharp knife, cut the terrine into slices and serve garnished with lemon wedges and fresh dill or fennel.

**Cook's tip** If you cannot find fromage blanc, substitute it with low-fat soft cream cheese.

*Below Boats moored on the tranquil waters of the Kenmare River, Ring of Kerry, County Kerry.*

Per portion Energy 290kcal/1216kJ; Protein 32.5g; Carbohydrate 13.7g, of which sugars 2.8g; Fat 12.1g, of which saturates 3.9g; Cholesterol 112mg; Calcium 203mg; Fibre 1.5g; Sodium 306mg

# Fish and shellfish

As an island nation, the Irish prize fish and shellfish as specialities, and these foods are much appreciated by residents and visitors alike. Dublin Bay prawns (jumbo shrimp), Galway oysters, wild salmon from the great fishing rivers and loughs, Wexford mussels, lobster and crab from all around the coast are among the many treats in store, presented in both traditional and creative modern dishes.

# Seafood pie

A well-made fish pie is absolutely delicious, and is particularly good made with a mixture of fresh and smoked fish – ideal winter fare when the fishing fleets are hampered by gales and fresh fish is in short supply. Cooked shellfish, such as mussels, can be included too.

**Serves 4–5**

450g/1lb haddock or cod fillet

225g/8oz smoked haddock or cod

150ml/¼ pint/⅔ cup milk

150ml/¼ pint/⅔ cup water

1 slice of lemon

1 small bay leaf

a few fresh parsley stalks

**For the sauce**

25g/1oz/2 tbsp butter

25g/1oz/¼ cup plain (all-purpose) flour

5ml/1 tbsp lemon juice, or to taste

45ml/3 tbsp chopped fresh parsley

ground black pepper

**For the topping**

450g/1lb potatoes, boiled and mashed

25g/1oz/2 tbsp butter

*Below* Sunset over the Blasket Islands, Inishtooskert, County Kerry.

**1** Preheat the oven to 190°C/375°F/Gas 5. Rinse the fish, cut it into manageable pieces and put into a pan with the milk, water, lemon, bay leaf and parsley stalks. Bring slowly to the boil, then simmer gently for 15 minutes until tender.

**2** Strain, reserving 300ml/½ pint/1¼ cups of the cooking liquor. Leave the fish until cool, then flake the flesh and discard the skin and bones. Set aside.

**3** To make the sauce, melt the butter in a heavy pan, add the flour and cook for 1–2 minutes over low heat stirring constantly. Then gradually add the reserved cooking liquor, stirring well to make a smooth sauce.

**4** Simmer the sauce gently for 1–2 minutes, then remove from the heat and stir in the flaked fish, chopped parsley and lemon juice. Season to taste with ground black pepper.

**5** Turn into a buttered 1.75 litre/3 pint/7½ cup pie dish or shallow casserole, cover with the mashed potato for the topping and dot with the butter.

**6** Cook in the oven for about 20 minutes, or until thoroughly heated through. The top should be golden brown and crunchy. Divide the pie among 4–5 warmed plates and serve with a lightly cooked green vegetable, such as fresh broccoli spears.

**Per portion** Energy 336kcal/1413kJ; Protein 35.1g; Carbohydrate 24.3g, of which sugars 0.9g; Fat 11.6g, of which saturates 6.7g; Cholesterol 87mg; Calcium 45mg; Fibre 1.7g; Sodium 587mg

# Dublin lawyer

This traditional dish used to be made with raw lobster, but it is now more usually lightly boiled first. The origins of the name are uncertain, but it is generally thought to refer to the fact that lawyers are more likely than most to be able to afford this luxurious dish.

**Serves 2**

1 large (over 900g/2lb), lightly cooked lobster (see Cook's tip)

175g/6oz/³⁄₄ cup butter

75ml/2¹⁄₂fl oz/¹⁄₃ cup Irish whiskey

150ml/¹⁄₄ pint/²⁄₃ cup double (heavy) cream

salt and ground black pepper, to taste

▶ **1** Tear off the claws from the cooked lobster. Split the body in half lengthways, with a sharp knife, just slightly to the right of the centre line to avoid cutting into the digestive tract. Remove the grey matter from the head of the shell and discard. Remove the digestive tract right down the length of the body and discard. Lift the flesh from the tail – it usually comes out in one piece. Set the shells aside for serving and keep them warm.

**2** Tear the two joints in the claw to separate them and, using a small knife, scoop out the flesh. With the back of a heavy knife, hit the claw near the pincers, rotating the claw and hitting until the claw opens. Remove the flesh and cut into bitesize pieces.

**3** Melt the butter in a pan over a low heat. Add the lobster pieces and turn in the butter to warm through. Warm the whiskey in a separate pan and pour it over the lobster. Carefully set it alight. Add the cream and heat gently without allowing the sauce to boil, then season to taste. Turn the hot mixture into the warm shells and serve immediately.

**Cook's tip** To cook, weigh the live lobster and put it into a pan of boiling salted water. Bring back to the boil and cook for 12 minutes per 450g/1lb for small lobsters, a little less if 900g/2lb or over. Remove the cooked lobster from the water and leave to cool.

Per portion Energy 1273kcal/5259kJ; Protein 37.8g; Carbohydrate 1.8g, of which sugars 1.8g; Fat 114.9g, of which saturates 71.1g; Cholesterol 469mg; Calcium 152mg; Fibre 0g; Sodium 1.08g

# Dublin Bay prawns in garlic butter

Although they are caught in the Irish Sea, Dublin Bay prawns are in fact the ubiquitous 'scampi'. This all-time favourite is equally popular as an appetizer or a light main course. Serve simply, with lemon wedges, rice and a green side salad.

**Serves 4**

32–36 large live Dublin Bay prawns (jumbo shrimp)

225g/8oz/1 cup butter

15ml/1 tbsp olive oil

4 or 5 garlic cloves, crushed

sea salt and ground black pepper

15ml/1 tbsp lemon juice

**1** Drop the live Dublin Bay prawns into a large pan of briskly boiling salted water. Bring rapidly back to the boil, cover with a lid and simmer for a few minutes; the time required depends on their size and will be very short for small ones – do not overcook. They are ready when the underside of the shell has lost its translucency and becomes an opaque whitish colour.

**2** Drain, refresh under cold water, and leave in a colander until cool. Twist off the heads and the long claws, then peel the shell off the tails and remove the meat. If the claws are big it is worthwhile extracting any meat you can from them with a lobster pick.

**3** Make a shallow cut along the back of each prawn. Remove the trail (the dark vein) that runs along the back.

**4** Heat a large heavy pan over medium heat, add the butter and oil and the garlic. When the butter is foaming, sprinkle the prawns with a little salt and a good grinding of pepper, and add them to the pan. Cook for about 2 minutes until the garlic is cooked and the prawns thoroughly heated through.

**5** Add lemon juice to taste, and adjust the seasoning, and then turn the prawns and their buttery juices on to warmed plates and serve immediately.

**Cook's tips**
• Dublin Bay prawns can weigh up to 225g/8oz each, although the average weight is 45g/1¾oz. You'll need 8–9 per person for a main course.
• These crustaceans are also known as Norway lobsters and langoustine.

**Variation** This recipe works very well with scallops (puréed Jerusalem artichokes are a good accompaniment), small queen scallops, or with a firm-fleshed fish such as monkfish.

**Per portion** Energy 498kcal/2054kJ; Protein 13g; Carbohydrate 0.4g, of which sugars 0.4g; Fat 49.4g, of which saturates 29.8g; Cholesterol 260mg; Calcium 67mg; Fibre 0g; Sodium 478mg

# Game pie

This country dish is adaptable and could be made with whatever game birds are available. Serve the pie with seasonal vegetables: potatoes boiled in their skins, puréed Jerusalem artichokes and winter greens, such as purple sprouting broccoli or Brussels sprouts.

**Serves 8–10**

4 pheasant and/or pigeon skinless breast portions

225g/8oz lean stewing steak

115g/4oz streaky (fatty) bacon, trimmed

butter, for frying

2 medium onions, finely chopped

1 large garlic clove, crushed

15ml/1 tbsp plain (all-purpose) flour

about 300ml/½ pint/¼ cup pigeon or pheasant stock

15ml/1 tbsp tomato purée (paste) (optional)

15ml/1 tbsp chopped fresh parsley

a little grated lemon rind

15ml/1 tbsp rowan or redcurrant jelly

50–115g/2–4oz button (white) mushrooms, halved or quartered if large

sea salt and ground black pepper

a small pinch of freshly grated nutmeg or ground loves (optional)

milk or beaten egg, to glaze

**For the rough-puff pastry**

225g/8oz/2 cups plain (all-purpose) flour

2.5ml/½ tsp salt

5ml/1 tsp lemon juice

115g/4oz/½ cup butter, in walnut-sized pieces

**1** To make the rough-puff pastry, sift the flour and salt into a large mixing bowl. Add the lemon juice and the butter pieces and just enough cold water to bind the ingredients together. Turn the mixture on to a floured board and roll the pastry into a long strip. Fold it into three and press the edges together. Half-turn the pastry, rib it with the rolling pin to equalize the air in it and roll it into a strip once again. Repeat this folding and rolling process three more times.

**2** Slice the pheasant or pigeon breasts from the bone and cut the meat into fairly thin strips. Trim away any fat from the stewing steak and slice it in the same manner. Cut the bacon into thin strips, and then cook it very gently in a heavy frying pan until the fat runs. Add some butter and brown the sliced pigeon or pheasant and stewing steak in it, a little at a time. Remove each batch when browned.

**3** Remove the meats from the pan and set aside. Cook the onions and garlic in the fat for 2–3 minutes over a medium heat. Remove and set aside with the meats, then stir the flour into the remaining fat. Cook for 1–2 minutes, and then gradually stir in enough stock to make a fairly thin gravy. Add the tomato purée, if using, parsley, lemon rind and rowan or redcurrant jelly and the mushrooms. Season to taste and add the nutmeg or cloves, if you like.

**4** Return the browned meats, chopped onion and garlic to the pan containing the gravy, and mix well before turning into a deep 1.75 litre/3 pint/7½ cup pie dish. Leave to cool. Meanwhile, preheat the oven to 220°C/425°F/Gas 7.

**5** Roll the prepared pastry out to make a circle 2.5cm/1in larger all round than the pie dish, and cut out to make a lid for the pie. Wet the rim of the pie dish and line with the remaining pastry strip. Dampen the strip and cover with the lid, pressing down well to seal.

**6** Trim away any excess pastry and knock up the edges with a knife. Make a hole in the centre for the steam to escape and use any pastry trimmings to decorate the top. Glaze the top of the pie with milk or beaten egg. Bake in the oven for about 20 minutes, until the pastry is well-risen, then reduce the oven to 150°C/300°F/Gas 2 for another 1½ hours, until cooked. Protect the pastry from over-browning if necessary by covering it with a double layer of wet baking parchment. Serve.

**Cook's tip** Frozen puff pastry could replace the home-made rough-puff pastry, if you prefer.

**Per portion** Energy 448kcal/1871kJ; Protein 28.3g; Carbohydrate 29.5g, of which sugars 5.3g; Fat 24.9g, of which saturates 9.5g; Cholesterol 55mg; Calcium 67mg; Fibre 1.5g; Sodium 393mg

# Roast loin of boar with poitín-soaked prunes

Farmed 'wild' boar is produced in Northern Ireland and tastes wonderful stuffed and roasted with black pudding mash, cooked cabbage and apple sauce. Whiskey can replace the poitín.

**Serves 4–6**

8 pitted prunes

1 glass poitín or Irish whiskey

675g/1½lb boned loin of boar, any excess fat removed

salt and ground black pepper

**1** Soak the prunes overnight in enough poitín or whiskey to cover.

**Cook's tip** To prepare the mash add 225g/8oz cooked black pudding to 1kg/2¼lb cooked potatoes. Mash well with cream and butter to taste. Stir in 15ml/1 tbsp mustard and season.

**2** Use a skewer to make a circular incision along the loin of boar and stuff with the prunes. Place a large square of foil on a flat surface. On top of the foil place a large square of clear film (plastic wrap). Place the loin on one end of the clear film and roll up tightly. Refrigerate for 2 hours.

**3** Preheat the oven to 200°C/400°F/ Gas 6. Remove the foil and clear film and cut the loin into tournedos (steaks). Preheat a heavy pan and sear the meat on both sides until brown. Season. Transfer to a roasting pan and cook in the oven for 7–10 minutes. Leave to rest before serving on heated plates.

**Per portion** Energy 2715kcal/11322kJ; Protein 274.9g; Carbohydrate 0g, of which sugars 0g; Fat 185.1g, of which saturates 67.7g; Cholesterol 964mg; Calcium 110mg; Fibre 0g; Sodium 894mg

# Home-made venison sausages

Venison sausages have an excellent flavour, a much lower fat content than most sausages and they're easy to make. The only tricky bit, obtaining and filling sausage skins, is omitted.

**Makes 1.4kg/3lb**

900g/2lb finely minced (ground) venison

450g/1lb finely minced (ground) belly of pork

15ml/1 tbsp salt

10ml/2 tsp ground black pepper

1 garlic clove, crushed

5ml/1 tsp dried thyme

1 egg, beaten

plain (all-purpose) flour, for dusting

vegetable oil, for frying

mashed potatoes, fried onions, grilled (broiled) or fried field (portabello) mushrooms and grilled tomatoes, to serve

**1** Combine all the ingredients, except the flour and oil, in a bowl. Take a small piece of the mixture and fry it in a little oil in a heavy frying pan, then taste to check the seasoning for the batch. Adjust if necessary.

**2** Form the mixture into chipolata-size sausages using floured hands.

**3** Heat the oil in a large, heavy frying pan and shallow-fry the sausages for 10 minutes or until they are golden brown and cooked right through.

**4** Serve with creamy mashed potatoes, fried onions, and grilled (broiled) mushrooms and tomatoes.

**Cook's tip** Venison sausages also freeze well if stored in an airtight container.

*Right A large herd of fallow deer grazing in the evening sun at Phoenix Park, Dublin.*

**Per portion** Energy 2715kcal/11322kJ; Protein 274.9g; Carbohydrate 0g, of which sugars 0g; Fat 185.1g, of which saturates 67.7g; Cholesterol 964mg; Calcium 110mg; Fibre 0g; Sodium 894mg

# Vegetable dishes

The wide range of vegetables enjoyed in Ireland today is a modern trend – most gardeners just grew simple vegetables like potatoes and cabbage until relatively recently. Now, however, Irish farmers, gardeners and cooks are making up for lost time and making the most of a surge of interest in vegetables, both traditional and more exotic.

# Leeks in cream sauce

This versatile vegetable makes a great winter standby and leeks find their way into many dishes, including casseroles and soups. Simple buttered leeks are underrated as a side dish, and this recipe makes a tasty accompaniment for plain grilled food, such as chops or chicken, or it can be served as a light lunch or supper on its own.

**Serves 4–6**

4 large or 8 medium leeks

salt and ground black pepper

300ml/½ pint/1¼ cups milk

8 streaky (fatty) rashers (strips) of bacon, trimmed and sliced (optional)

1 egg, lightly beaten

150ml/¼ pint/⅔ cup single (light) cream

15ml/1 tbsp mild Irish mustard

75g/3oz/¾ cup grated cheese (optional)

**1** Slice the leeks into fairly large chunks. Put them into a pan with the milk. Season and bring to the boil. Reduce the heat and simmer for 15–20 minutes, or until tender. Drain well and turn the leeks into a buttered shallow baking dish, reserving the cooking liquor.

**2** Meanwhile, if using the bacon, put it into a frying pan and cook gently to allow the fat to run, then turn up the heat a little and cook for a few minutes until it crisps up. Remove from the pan with a slotted spoon and sprinkle the bacon over the leeks.

**3** Rinse the pan used for the leeks. Blend the beaten egg, single cream and Irish mustard together and mix it with the reserved cooking liquor.

**4** Return the egg mixture to the pan and heat gently over low heat without boiling, allowing the sauce to thicken a little.

**5** Taste and adjust the seasoning as necessary with salt and freshly ground black pepper. Pour the sauce over the leeks and bacon.

**6** Sprinkle with grated cheese, if using, and brown for a few minutes under a hot grill (broiler). (Alternatively, the leeks may served immediately without browning.)

**7** Serve with plain grilled meat or poultry, if you like.

**Variation** The bacon may be grilled and served separately, if you prefer.

**Per portion** Energy 238kcal/993kJ; Protein 18.6g; Carbohydrate 9g, of which sugars 7.9g; Fat 14.4g, of which saturates 7.3g; Cholesterol 90mg; Calcium 172mg; Fibre 3.5g; Sodium 830mg

# Baked onions

One of Ireland's oldest and most widely used flavouring vegetables, the onion also deserves to be used more as a vegetable in its own right. Onions become sweet and mildly flavoured when boiled or baked, and can be cooked very conveniently in the oven with just a little water when baking potatoes or parsnips to make a delicious side dish.

**Serves 4**

**4 large even-sized onions**

**Cook's tip** These onions are baked in their skins, but you could peel them, if preferred, before baking. The peeled onions are best baked in a covered casserole dish instead of a roasting tin.

◀ **1** Preheat the oven to 180°C/350°F/ Gas 4. Put a little cold water into a medium-size roasting pan, and arrange the unpeeled onions in it.

**2** Bake in the preheated oven for about 1 hour, or until the onions feel soft when squeezed at the sides. Peel the skins and serve immediately.

**Per portion** Energy 90kcal/375kJ; Protein 3g; Carbohydrate 19.8g, of which sugars 14g; Fat 0.5g, of which saturates 0g; Cholesterol 0mg; Calcium 63mg; Fibre 3.5g; Sodium 8mg

# Desserts and baking

Good home baking has always been one of the great
strengths of Irish cooking, be it the simple soda breads
and delectable cakes for which Ireland is renowned or
comforting desserts based on country ingredients such as
home-grown apples and pears, cottage garden summer
fruits such as rhubarb, blackcurrants and strawberries – and
wild berries, including blackberries and bilberries.

# Fraughan mousse

Wild or cottage-garden fruits, or a combination of both, have long been used to make simple desserts such as mousses, creams and fools. This bilberry dish is an attractive and impressive finish for a dinner party. Serve chilled with whipped cream and sponge fingers.

**Serves 6–8**

450g/1lb cooking apples

450g/1lb/4 cups fraughans (bilberries)

115g/4oz/generous ½ cup caster (superfine) sugar

juice of 1 lemon

1 sachet powdered gelatine

2 egg whites

60ml/4 tbsp double (heavy) cream, to serve

**1** Peel, core and slice the apples, then put them into a pan with the fraughans (bilberries), 150ml/¼ pint/⅔ cup water and 75g/3oz/scant ½ cup of the sugar.

**2** Cook gently for 15 minutes, until the berries are tender. Remove the pan from the heat.

**3** Strain the lemon juice into a cup, sprinkle the gelatine over and leave it to soak. Add the cake of soaked gelatine to the fruit and stir until it has dissolved. Turn into a nylon sieve over a large mixing bowl and press the fruit through it to make a purée; discard anything that is left in the sieve. Leave the purée to stand until it is cool and beginning to set.

**4** Whisk the egg whites stiffly, sprinkle in the remaining sugar and whisk again until glossy. Using a metal spoon, fold the whites gently into the fruit purée to make a smooth mousse. Turn into serving glasses and chill until set. Serve topped with double cream.

**Variation** Bilberries, also known as whortleberries and by their Irish name, *fraughans*, grow prolifically in bogs and moorland areas all over Ireland in late summer, and bilberry picking makes a great family day out. This modern recipe stretches a modest amount of wild fruit, and can be used to make a mousse with other soft summer fruits, notably the bilberry's larger cultivated cousin, the blueberry, and it works equally well with blackberries.

**Per portion** Energy 118kcal/498kJ; Protein 1.9g; Carbohydrate 28.7g, of which sugars 28.7g; Fat 0.2g, of which saturates 0g; Cholesterol 0mg; Calcium 44mg; Fibre 3.2g; Sodium 24mg

# Irish whiskey trifle

This luxuriously rich trifle is made the old-fashioned way, with real sponge cake, fresh fruit and rich egg custard, but with Irish whiskey rather than the usual sherry flavouring. A good egg custard is essential, so don't be tempted to use a convenient alternative.

**Serves 6–8**

1 x 15–18cm/6–7in sponge cake

225g/8oz raspberry jam

150ml/¼ pint/⅔ cup whiskey

450g/1lb ripe fruit, such as pears and bananas

300ml/½ pint/1¼ cups whipping cream, whipped

blanched almonds, glacé cherries and angelica, to decorate (optional)

**For the custard**

450ml/¾ pint/scant 2 cups full cream (whole) milk

1 vanilla pod (bean) or a few drops of vanilla extract

3 eggs

25g/1oz/2 tbsp caster (superfine) sugar

**1** To make the custard, put the milk into a pan with the vanilla pod, if using, and bring almost to the boil. Remove from the heat. Whisk the eggs and sugar together. Remove the pod. Gradually whisk the milk into the egg mixture.

**Variation** Good-quality canned fruit can be used instead of fresh fruit.

**2** Rinse out the pan with cold water, return the mixture to it and stir over low heat until it thickens enough to cover the back of a wooden spoon; do not allow the custard to boil. Alternatively, for a very slow method of cooking, use a double boiler, or a bowl over a pan of boiling water.

**3** Turn the custard into a mixing bowl and add the vanilla extract, if using. Cover the custard and set aside until ready to assemble the trifle.

**4** Halve the sponge cake horizontally, spread with the raspberry jam and make a sandwich. Using a sharp knife cut into slices and use them to line the bottom and lower sides of a large glass serving bowl.

**5** Sprinkle with the whiskey. Peel and slice the fruit, then spread it out over the sponge in an even layer. Pour the custard on top, cover with clear film (plastic wrap) and leave to cool and set. Chill until required.

**6** Before serving, spread the cream over the custard. Decorate with the almonds, glacé cherries and angelica, if you like.

**Per portion** Energy 710kcal/2959kJ; Protein 12.1g; Carbohydrate 58g, of which sugars 42.6g; Fat 43.2g, of which saturates 14.4g; Cholesterol 171mg; Calcium 194mg; Fibre 2.3g; Sodium 336mg

# Bailey's carrageen pudding

Carrageen, also known as Irish moss, is a purplish variety of seaweed that is found all along the west coast of Ireland. Carrageen pudding is an old-fashioned set milk dessert that is still widely made. This version is made with Bailey's Irish Cream and would be a good choice for a dessert selection at a party or buffet.

**Serves 8–10**

15g/½oz carrageen

1.5 litres/2½ pints/6¼ cups milk

300ml/½ pint/1¼ cups Bailey's Irish Cream

2 eggs, separated

about 60ml/4 tbsp caster (superfine) sugar

**1** Soak the carrageen in tepid water for 10 minutes. Put the milk into a pan with the drained carrageen. Bring to the boil and simmer very gently for 20 minutes, stirring occasionally.

**2** Strain the mixture and rub all the jelly through the sieve; discard anything remaining in it. Rinse out the pan and return the mixture to it, over a very low heat. Blend in the Bailey's.

**3** Heat the mixture very gently to just below boiling point, and then remove from the heat.

**4** Mix the egg yolks and the sugar together and blend in a little of the hot mixture, then stir, or whisk, the egg yolks and sugar into the hot mixture. When the sugar has dissolved, leave the mixture to cool a little, and then whisk the egg whites stiffly and fold in gently.

**5** Turn into a serving bowl and leave in the refrigerator to set. Serve alone, or with a dessert selection.

**Variation** Replace the Bailey's with the same amount of milk for a plain dish, and use as an alternative to cream with desserts, such as poached fruit.

**Cook's tip** When dried, carrageen is a good thickening agent for puddings, ice cream and soups.

**Per portion** Energy 260kcal/1090kJ; Protein 8.3g; Carbohydrate 25.2g, of which sugars 25.2g; Fat 10.7g, of which saturates 2.5g; Cholesterol 68mg; Calcium 0.2g; Fibre 0g; Sodium 0.1g

# Brown bread ice cream

The secret of a good brown bread ice cream is not to have too many breadcrumbs (which makes the ice cream heavy) and, for the best texture and deep, nutty flavour, to toast them until really crisp and well browned. Yeast bread produces a better flavour than soda bread for this recipe. Serve the ice cream either on its own or with a chocolate or fruit sauce.

**Serves 6–8**

115g/4oz/2 cups wholemeal (whole-wheat) breadcrumbs

115g/4oz/½ cup soft brown sugar

2 large (US extra large) eggs, separated

30–45ml/2–3 tbsp Irish Cream liqueur

450ml/¾ pint/scant 2 cups double (heavy) cream

**1** Preheat the oven to 190°C/375°F/ Gas 5. Spread the breadcrumbs out on a baking sheet and toast them in the oven for about 15 minutes, or until crisp and well browned. Leave to cool.

**2** Whisk the sugar and egg yolks together until light and creamy, then beat in the Irish Cream. Whisk the cream until soft peaks form. In a separate bowl, whisk the egg whites stiffly.

◄ **3** Sprinkle the breadcrumbs over the beaten egg mixture, add the cream and fold into the mixture with a spoon. Fold in the beaten egg whites. Turn the mixture into a freezerproof container, cover and freeze.

***Right*** *The popular holiday destination of Ventry, County Kerry.*

**Per portion** Energy 561kcal/2332kJ; Protein 6g; Carbohydrate 37.3g, of which sugars 23g; Fat 43.6g, of which saturates 25.7g; Cholesterol 179mg; Calcium 84mg; Fibre 0.4g; Sodium 196mg

# Brown soda bread

Soda bread is best eaten on the day of baking, but it slices better if left to cool and 'set' on a wire rack for several hours. It is delicious with good butter, farmhouse cheese and some crisp sticks of celery or a bowl of home-made soup.

**Makes 1 loaf**

450g/1lb/4 cups wholemeal (whole-wheat) flour

175g/6oz/1½ cups plain (all-purpose) flour

7.5ml/1½ tsp bicarbonate of soda (baking soda)

5ml/1 tsp salt

about 450ml/¾ pint/scant 2 cups buttermilk

**Variation** Cream of tartar can be added to the dry ingredients to provide the acid instead of buttermilk.

**1** Preheat the oven to 200°C/400°F/ Gas 6, and grease a baking sheet. Combine the dry ingredients in a mixing bowl and stir in enough buttermilk to make a fairly soft dough. Turn on to a work surface dusted with wholemeal flour and knead lightly until smooth.

**2** Form the dough into a circle, about 4cm/1½in thick. Lay on the baking sheet and mark a deep cross in the top with a floured knife.

**3** Bake for about 45 minutes, or until the bread is browned and sounds hollow when tapped on the base. Cool on a wire rack. If a soft crust is preferred, wrap the loaf in a clean dishtowel while cooling.

***Above*** *The beautiful landscape of the river and valleys of Killorglin and Glenbeigh, County Kerry.*

Per loaf Energy 2262kcal/9643kJ; Protein 88.5g; Carbohydrate 465.4g, of which sugars 31.4g; Fat 18.9g, of which saturates 6.5g; Cholesterol 27mg; Calcium 1.37g; Fibre 34.2g; Sodium 2.18g

# Oven-baked potato cakes

Potato cakes are widely made in Ireland and come in a variety of forms, but they're all at their best if made with freshly cooked potatoes, preferably while still warm. Serve straight from the oven, split open and buttered while hot.

**Makes about 12**

225g/8oz/2 cups self-raising (self-rising) flour

2.5ml/½ tsp baking powder

50g/2oz/¼ cup butter, diced

a pinch of salt

175g/6oz freshly cooked mashed potato

15ml/1 tbsp chopped fresh chives

200ml/7fl oz/scant 1 cup buttermilk

**1** Preheat the oven to 220°C/425°F/ Gas 7 and lightly grease a baking tray with butter.

**2** Sift the flour and the baking powder into a bowl and rub in the butter. Season with salt. Add the mashed potato and chives. Mix well, and then incorporate enough buttermilk to make a soft dough. Turn on to a floured work surface, knead lightly into shape then quickly roll out.

**3** Cut into squares with a sharp floured knife or stamp out into rounds with a 5cm/2in cutter.

**4** Place on the baking tray and bake in the preheated oven for about 20 minutes or until well risen, golden brown and crisp.

**Per cake** Energy 108kcal/455kJ; Protein 2g; Carbohydrate 16.5g, of which sugars 0.4g; Fat 4.3g, of which saturates 2.6g; Cholesterol 11mg; Calcium 68mg; Fibre 0.7g; Sodium 99mg

# Quick barm brack

The traditional yeasted barm brack is mainly associated with Halloween and contains all kinds of symbolic tokens, of which the best known is the ring (signifying marriage within the year for the recipient). This is a simplified version of the yeasted brack, made with easy-blend yeast.

**Makes 2 loaves**

450g/1lb/4 cups plain (all-purpose) flour

5ml/1 tsp mixed (apple pie) spice

2.5ml/½ tsp salt

2 sachets easy-blend (rapid-rise) dried yeast

75g/3oz/6 tbsp soft dark brown sugar

115g/4oz/½ cup butter, melted

300ml/½ pint/1¼ cups tepid milk

1 egg, lightly beaten

375g/13oz/generous 2 cups dried mixed fruit

25g/1oz/⅓ cup chopped mixed (candied) peel

15ml/1 tbsp caster (superfine) sugar

**1** Butter two 450g/1lb loaf tins (pans). Mix the flour, spice, salt, yeast and sugar in a large bowl and make a well in the centre. Mix the butter with the tepid milk and egg and add to the bowl.

**2** Add the mixed fruit and peel and mix well. Turn the mixture into the loaf tins. Leave in a warm place for about 30 minutes to rise. Meanwhile, preheat the oven to 200°C/400°F/Gas 6.

**3** When the dough has doubled in size, bake for about 45 minutes, or until the loaves begin to shrink from the sides of the tins; when turned out and rapped underneath they should sound hollow.

**4** Make a glaze by mixing the sugar with 30ml/2 tbsp boiling water. Remove the loaves from the oven and brush over with the glaze. Return them to the oven for 3 minutes, or until the tops are a rich shiny brown. Turn on to a wire rack to cool.

**Per loaf** Energy 2019kcal/8524kJ; Protein 34.9g; Carbohydrate 364.6g, of which sugars 193.2g; Fat 57g, of which saturates 32.8g; Cholesterol 246mg; Calcium 704mg; Fibre 11.7g; Sodium 590mg

# Irish apple cake

This moist cake – also known as Kerry apple cake in the south of the country – is perhaps best in autumn, when home-grown apples are in season. It has a lovely crunchy top and can be served cold, as a cake, or warm with chilled cream or custard as a dessert.

**Makes 1 cake**

225g/8oz/2 cups self-raising (self-rising) flour

good pinch of salt

pinch of ground cloves

115g/4oz/½ cup butter, at room temperature

3 or 4 cooking apples, such as Bramley's Seedling

115g/4oz/generous ½ cup caster (superfine) sugar

2 eggs, beaten

a little milk to mix

granulated sugar to sprinkle over

**1** Preheat the oven to 190°C/375°F/Gas 5 and butter a 20cm/8in cake tin (pan).

**2** Sift the flour, salt and ground cloves into a bowl. Cut in the butter and rub in until the mixture is like fine breadcrumbs. Peel and core the apples. Slice them thinly and add to the rubbed in mixture with the sugar.

**3** Mix in the eggs and enough milk to make a fairly stiff dough, then turn the mixture into the prepared tin and sprinkle with granulated sugar.

**4** Bake in the preheated oven for 30–40 minutes, or until springy to the touch. Cool on a wire rack. Store in an airtight container until ready to serve.

**Per cake** Energy 2315kcal/9717kJ; Protein 37g; Carbohydrate 312.5g, of which sugars 145.3g; Fat 110.9g, of which saturates 64.1g; Cholesterol 702mg; Calcium 948mg; Fibre 10.7g; Sodium 1.68g

# Porter cake

Porter was a key ingredient in many traditional Irish dishes, both sweet and savoury, adding colour and richness of flavour without being over-dominant. Stout is a good substitute in recipes like this one, although it is sometimes better diluted.

**Makes 1 20cm/8in round cake**

225g/8oz/1 cup butter, at room temperature

225g/8oz/1 cup soft dark brown sugar

350g/12oz/3 cups plain (all-purpose) flour

pinch of salt

5ml/1 tsp baking powder

5ml/1 tsp mixed (apple pie) spice

3 eggs

450g/1lb/2⅓ cups mixed dried fruit

115g/4oz/½ cup glacé (candied) cherries

115g/4oz/⅔ cup mixed (candied) peel

50g/2oz/½ cup chopped almonds or walnuts

about 150ml/¼ pint/⅔ cup stout, such as Guinness

**1** Preheat the oven to 160°C/325°F/Gas 3. Grease and base line a 20cm/8in round deep cake tin (pan).

**2** Cream the butter and sugar in a bowl, until light and fluffy. Sift the flour, salt, baking powder and spice into another bowl.

**3** Add the eggs to the butter and sugar mixture, one at a time, adding a little of the flour mixture with each egg and beating well after each addition. Mix well and blend in any remaining flour. Add the fruit and nuts and enough stout to make quite a soft consistency. Mix well.

**4** Turn the mixture into the prepared tin and bake in the preheated oven for 1 hour. Reduce the heat to 150°C/300°F/Gas 2 and cook for a further 1½–2 hours, or until the top is firm to the touch and a skewer pushed into the centre comes out clean. Cool the cake in the tin.

**5** When cold, remove the lining paper, wrap in fresh baking parchment and store in an airtight container for at least a week before eating.

**Cook's tip** Porter cake is made by many methods, ranging from rubbed-in tea-breads to the creaming method, as here.

Per cake Energy 6130kcal/25807kJ; Protein 80.2g; Carbohydrate 964.9g, of which sugars 696.9g; Fat 240.2g, of which saturates 125.7g; Cholesterol 1.16g; Calcium 1.42mg; Fibre 31g; Sodium 2.23g

# Irish whiskey cake

This light, moist cake has the subtle flavours of lemon and cloves, rather like hot Irish whiskey – making it seem especially tempting in winter. The tangy icing and slices of crystallized lemon contrast perfectly with the rich, crumbly cake.

**Makes 1 18cm/7in round cake**

225g/8oz/1⅓ cups sultanas (golden raisins)

grated rind of 1 lemon

150ml/¼ pint/⅔ cup Irish or other good-quality whiskey

175g/6oz/¾ cup unsalted butter, softened

175g/6oz/¾ cup soft light brown sugar

175g/6oz/1½ cups plain (all-purpose) flour

pinch of salt

1.5ml/¼ tsp ground cloves

5ml/1 tsp baking powder

3 large (US extra large) eggs, separated

**For the icing**

juice of 1 lemon

225g/8oz/2 cups icing (confectioners') sugar

crystallized lemon slices, to decorate (optional)

**1** Put the sultanas and grated lemon rind into a small bowl with the whiskey, cover with clear film (plastic wrap) and leave overnight to soak.

**2** Preheat the oven to 180°C/350°F/Gas 4. Grease and base line a loose-based 18cm/7in deep cake tin (pan).

**3** Cream the butter and sugar together until light and fluffy. Sift the flour, salt, cloves and baking powder together into a bowl.

**4** Beat the yolks into the butter and sugar one at a time, adding a little of the flour with each egg and beating well after each addition.

**5** Gradually blend in the sultana and whiskey mixture, alternating with the remaining flour. Do not overbeat the mixture at this stage.

**6** Whisk the egg whites until stiff and fold them into the mixture with a metal spoon. Turn the mixture into the prepared tin and bake in the preheated oven for 1½ hours, or until the top is firm to the touch and a skewer pushed into the centre comes out clean. Turn out and cool on a rack.

**7** Meanwhile, make the icing: mix the lemon juice with the icing sugar and enough warm water to make a pouring consistency. Lay a plate under the cake rack to catch the drips and pour the icing over a spoonful at a time, letting it dribble down the sides. Any icing dripping on to the plate may be put on top again. When the icing has set, it can be decorated with lemon slices, if you like.

**Per cake** Energy 4691kcal/19,730kJ; Protein 48.1g; Carbohydrate 711.2g, of which sugars 577.8g; Fat 167g, of which saturates 97.1g; Cholesterol 1.06g; Calcium 735mg; Fibre 9.9g; Sodium 1.38g

# Index